Reflections of the Cotswolds

MORE COUNTRY FOLK

COUNTRY WAYS

Photographs by Betty Stocker   **Words by Tooty Gibbs**

Dedicated to Jim Stocker.

Thanks to all the people featured; without their co-operation this book would not have been possible.

ISBN 978-0-9565284-1-4

Published by Betty Stocker © 2016

**Book and original photographs available from
www.bettystocker.com**

Introduction

Betty Stocker is a true countrywoman, born in rural Cotswolds, brought up to appreciate its traditions and its natural beauty.

Her photography reflects her love of all things country, and communicates her knowledge of the area as a real, working, breathing environment.

This second book again records in skilful, artistic detail, a way of life which many may think no longer exists; however Betty has sought out and photographed a whole range of thriving country pursuits, recording expertise, pastimes and traditions passed down through generations.

But perhaps Betty's first love is in capturing those idyllic, atmospheric, pastoral scenes which are revealed at every twist and turn of the winding Cotswold lanes, and they too are reproduced in this book.

Tooty Gibbs grew up on a South Warwickshire farm and enjoyed an enviable childhood in the days when cows really were called Buttercup or Daisy, the hens laid their eggs in the nooks and crannies of the haybarn, and the meadows were brimming with bee orchids and cranesbill, sorrel and toadflax, moon daisies and scabious....

Her continued hope is that the present generation of children will in turn be able to look back on the infinite beauty of the countryside with the same degree of nostalgia.

The imminent reawakening of the seasons beckons us in to explore this beautiful creation which surrounds us ....

Snowdrops at the Rococo Garden at Painswick herald the end of winter and symbolise the beginning of something new.

Already now the snowdrop dares appear,
The first pale blossom of the unripened year;
As Flora's breath, by some transforming power,
Had changed an icicle into a flower.
Anna Laetitia Barbauld

A carpet of wood anemones at Westonbirt Arboretum unfolds beneath these mature hazel trees. The wood anemone is one of the earliest and prettiest of all woodland flowers. Its common names include windflower, thimbleweed, lady's nightcap, moonflower, old woman's nest, wood crowfoot, and smell fox – an allusion to the musky smell of the leaves. As a species it is surprisingly slow to spread (six feet in a hundred years!), relying on the growth of its root structure rather than the spread of its seed. As such, it is a good indicator of ancient woodland. It is poisonous to humans.

COPPICING

Forestry managers at Westonbirt are running a Coppice Restoration Project, planning to bring 60 acres of woodland back into coppice production; this includes large areas of hazel which have become overgrown.

Coppicing as a traditional method of woodland management has been in decline for a couple of hundred years but is now finding favour again. The process involves cutting the trees down to stumps in Winter: this promotes new growth, encourages the tree to live longer, and resulting improved light levels stimulate biodiversity on the woodland floor. The whole process is repeated about every seven years, ensuring a regular supply of wood.

Over a period of years the regrowth can be pleached, or layered, to produce more saplings. Here, in Spring, some of the bark has been scraped from the branches which have then been pegged down into a shallow earth trench where they will take root and begin a new tree.

The harvested wood is used to make hurdles, fencing, roof shingles, pea sticks, bean poles etc.

Charcoal is made from the harvested hardwoods: hazel, oak, ash, and birch is loaded into kilns, with no chemical additives, and charred for 24 hours.

A stunning vermilion sunrise over Goose Hill, Charingworth.

Throughout March and April, hosts of wild daffodils drift through the damp meadows, woodlands and orchards around Kempley. Also known as the Lenten Lily, the wild daffodil is smaller and has paler petals than the garden variety. It is the county flower of Gloucestershire.

Quintessential Cotswolds.

The year's at the spring and day's at the morn;
Morning's at seven; the hillside's dew-pearled;
The lark's on the wing; the snail's on the thorn;
God's in His Heaven; all's right with the world!

Robert Browning

This dazzling sea of bluebells sparkles in the Spring sunshine filtering through the canopy of beech and oaks in the ancient Evenlode wood. Since beech bark is extremely thin and scars easily, carvings such as lovers' initials remain visible for many years because the tree is unable to heal itself.

SKYLARK PLOTS

The patches of bare soil visible on this hillside field of Winter wheat were deliberately created when the farmer was planting the seed, in order to provide feeding grounds for skylarks.

Skylark populations have dropped dramatically over recent years, mainly due to the fact that farmers generally have switched from Spring to Autumn sown cereals – skylarks are ground-nesting birds, and because the Autumn sown vegetation is taller and thicker by the time of the breeding season it is rarely suitable for rearing more than one brood. In addition the absence of the stubble which would have been produced from Spring grown crops results in a lack of favourite feeding areas.

However, this wildlife-friendly farming initiative provides a good source of food for the birds: weeds grow in the bare patches and the skylarks can then forage for seeds and insects in the open soil.

This approach has been shown to increase the number of chicks successfully reared by about 50% since they are better fed and therefore more likely to survive Winter.

A further advantage is that these plots benefit plants and invertebrates.

A skylark's nest

FARM SUNDAY

The annual Farm Sunday service at Burhill Farm celebrates the agricultural year.

Buckland village, a Cotswolds gem tucked away in a secluded hollow at the foot of Burhill.

This well-worn track winds up to the barns on the top of Burhill where the service will take place.

The light soils of the high uplands ensure good sheep pasture.

Blessing the plough and seed.

On behalf of the farming community, local farmer John Hutcheon asks the Reverend John Newcombe to bestow God's blessing on the plough, the seed, and the Jacob sheep. The congregation responds with prayers of thanksgiving for all the gifts of Nature.

The benediction is pronounced from the steps of the combine harvester.

After the service the gathering enjoys a welcome cup of tea and some delicious home-made cakes....

The Market Hall on the High Street in Chipping Campden was built in 1627 by Sir Baptist Hicks, the wealthy benefactor who was responsible for many of the town's fine buildings. Its purpose was to provide shelter for local traders selling poultry, cheese and butter to the townsfolk. It was owned by the Noel family until 1942, when it was bought by the National Trust. It is still occasionally used by various tradespeople.

THE COTSWOLD LION

The high growth rate of the breed contributes to their increasing popularity.... amazingly these juveniles, or hoggets, are only a year old!

The white-faced Cotswold Lion sheep has been roaming the Cotswold hills since Roman times. By the end of WW1 only a few flocks remained but thanks to the work of conservationists this rare breed is flourishing again.

Their wool is known as the Golden Fleece, because in its heyday it made a major contribution to the wealth of the nation and of the development of many Cotswold towns and villages involved in processing the yarn. Their long fleece can make them appear somewhat comical at times!

Traditionally, a shepherd's coffin would be buried with a tuft of sheep's wool nailed to the lid - one thought being that St. Peter at the Pearly Gates would instantly recognise the arrival of a shepherd and consequently would ask no questions about non-attendance at church on Sundays!

ST. GEORGE'S DAY

Villagers at Ebrington enjoy a traditional roast beef lunch to celebrate St. George's Day.

Drinkwaters, the greengrocers in Chipping Campden, decorate their shop window in honour of our Patron Saint.

A striking bronze figure of St. George spearing a dragon dominates the war memorial at Stanway.

MAY DAY TRADITIONS

Children from St. James's School in Chipping Campden are up soon after daybreak on the 1st of May to take part in traditional maypole dancing in the Town Square. Proud parents, visitors, the Town Mayor and the Campden Morris Men are all there to lend encouragement and lead the applause.

Campden Morris Men have a history dating back to the 1700's: their dances and music are part of a living tradition passed from one generation to the next.

Guests at the nearby hotel have a bird's-eye view of this entertaining Stick Dance, performed with great gusto.

© Betty Stocker

In late April and early May the patchwork landscape is studded with the dazzling citrus yellow of rapeseed, and the air is filled with its distinctive heady aroma.

Wisteria, Broadway High Street.

The delicately scented pendant flowers of this stunning wisteria complement beautifully the honey tones of this Cotswold stone cottage.

BLESSING THE ANIMALS

Pets and their owners gather for a service of blessing at St. Andrew's Church, Aston Sub-Edge.

Can I come in?

Praying they will be on their best behaviour....

I couldn't bring my herd of cows but I do have this fabulous tie!

I'm not saying this sermon is boring....

Anyone up for a game of hide-and-seek? I'm too tired.

I know all the words!

LOWER CLOPTON FARM

Lower Clopton Farm Shop is a family-run business located at the foot of Meon Hill near Mickleton, established in 2004 as an extension to the farming business. Richard and Suzie Baldwyn sell top quality produce sourced from their own farm and other local farms, and they also provide a Farm Trail and Picnic Area where families can enjoy a fun and educational day out.

Contented Limousin and Belgian Blue cows and their calves find a shady spot.

Ewes and their lambs graze on the slopes of Meon Hill.

The Baldwyn family feed their free-range hens.

Collecting eggs – a favourite task for the next generation.

Richard picks damsons in the orchard, watched closely by a flock of inquisitive geese.

A tempting display of choice cheeses, gourmet pickles and preserves, and home-made puddings and pies in the farm shop.

There is always a wide selection of fresh seasonal fruit and vegetables available.

A full butchery service is on offer, with award-winning sausages, free-range poultry, and local game in season.

The lushness of the Summer garden complements the geese fattening in the neighbouring orchard at Lower Clopton.

SHIN KICKING

Shin kicking is not for the faint-hearted! It is one of the most popular events at the Cotswold Olimpick Games held annually on Dover's Hill. The two combatants grip each other by the shoulders and aim kicks to the shin in an attempt to force their opponent to the ground. The stickler, or referee, is there to see fair play: the winner is the best of three rounds. Competitors wear white coats to represent shepherds' smocks; they must wear soft shoes, and stuff their trouser legs with straw for padding. Success requires agility, but mostly the ability to withstand pain!

STREET FAIR

All the fun of a street fair follows the annual Scuttlebrook Wake in Chipping Campden. King Henry II granted Campden a Town Charter in about 1175, permitting a weekly market and annual fairs.

A tide of scarlet sweeps across the Snowshill escarpment.

"Through the dancing poppies stole
A breeze most softly lulling my soul"

John Keats, 'Endymion'

SHIPSTON WOOL FAIR

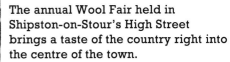
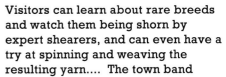

The annual Wool Fair held in Shipston-on-Stour's High Street brings a taste of the country right into the centre of the town.

Visitors can learn about rare breeds and watch them being shorn by expert shearers, and can even have a try at spinning and weaving the resulting yarn.... The town band entertains the crowds as they browse the many sheep-related stalls and sample the numerous delicious locally produced refreshments.

A brilliant day of education and entertainment, helping to keep alive the town's proud history as a "sheep wash" town!

SHEEP SHEARING

Sheep shearing and wool production have been an important part of the UK's sheep industry over the past 6000 years, especially in the Cotswolds. But nowadays wool prices are generally low and producers are lucky if they can recoup the cost of shearing.

Midsummer, and farmer Richard Baldwyn has corralled his sheep ready for shearing.

The blades are adjusted in readiness: a sharp cutting edge is essential to ensure the fleece can be removed cleanly and without stressing the animal.

Shearing is a specialised skill, and very hard work.... the aim is to get the job done in 2 - 3 minutes.

Elizabeth Baldwyn cleans any debris from the fleece before folding and rolling it neatly towards the neck end. She then twists and tucks the neck wool firmly into the bulk of the fleece.

The freshly shorn sheep look quite gaunt and exposed, but doubtless are feeling refreshed as they return to their pastures near Mickleton.

GUNDOGS

Ricky Moloney's Ribblesdale Labradors pay rapt attention and hang on his every command.

Ricky's wife Sandra makes learning fun for the Labrador pups but like all youngsters their concentration can lapse....

Ricky, from Lechlade, trains his Labradors to be gundogs and also schools them to compete in field trials.

Gundogs are used to retrieve dead and wounded game no matter where it lands. The only difference with field trials is a judge specifies which retrieve is required to be picked. A well trained dog should perform both tasks.

Ricky's dogs are trained in both disciplines.

As part of a campaign to promote the British Wool Industry, BBC Countryfile presenter Adam Henson takes to the streets of Stow-on-the-Wold to model a bespoke Savile Row suit which was made with wool from rare breeds of British sheep reared on his Cotswold Farm.

The stars of the show pause for a little window shopping....

SHEEP SHOWERING

Richard Smith arrives with his mobile Sheep Showering Unit at Terry and Maureen Booth's Sheepfolds Farm near Snowshill.

Meg Beck, from Winchcombe Young Farmers Club, helps Richard and shepherd Steve Hill set up the equipment.

Steve and Meg and friends round up the flock.

The trusty sheep dogs make sure there is no turning back....

Waiting in the barn.... they know who is in control!

Sheep are loaded twelve at a time into the shower pen.

Compulsory sheep dipping was withdrawn in 1989 but most sheep farmers still consider it prudent in order to eradicate the various parasites which bother sheep - lice, mites, blowflies, ticks etc.

Sheep showers have significant environmental advantages over dip baths as the amount of chemicals needed is kept to a minimum, and therefore there is less to dispose of. Showering also causes less stress to the sheep than total immersion.

The shower fluid - organophosphate - is pumped through the spray heads by an engine-powered pump. The high level spray douses the back of the fleece for 2½ minutes, and a floor-mounted spray wets the underside of the sheep for 30 seconds. The fluid drains off, and flows back to a sump where it is picked up and recirculated.

Drying off in the sunshine before going back to their pasture.

A breathtaking view of Buckland Church and the Buckland Manor Hotel, captured from Burhill.

St. Michael's Church, Buckland, dates from the 13th century. Although relatively small, it boasts a wealth of interesting artefacts, including a medieval holy water stoup, a 15th century panelled font, a 16th century mazer, painted stone panels, and the 15th century Buckland Cope, reputed to have come from Hailes Abbey at the Dissolution.

The high-backed shepherds' pews in the south aisle, complete with hat pegs, were located here so that shepherds and their dogs could enter the church via the west door and sit away from the rest of the congregation in their Sunday finery!

Much of the original panelling, the three-decker pulpit and the box pews were replaced in the church restoration of 1878. Some of the panelling was used to construct the current multi-sided pulpit.

John Wesley, the founder of Methodism, preached twice at Buckland in the 1720's - he and his brother Charles were frequent visitors to their friends at St. Michael and All Angel's Church at Stanton.... it's not hard to imagine them riding along the hill and down into the village....

The east window contains some beautiful 15th century stained glass panels, also reputedly from Hailes Abbey. In the 19th century William Morris, a major contributor to the Arts and Crafts Movement, attended services when he came to Buckland. Records show that he was so impressed with the window that he personally paid for and supervised its restoration.

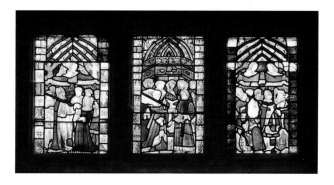

STANWAY ESTATE FLOUR MILL

The Stanway Estate Flour Mill, part of which dates from the 13th century, has undergone a ten year restoration programme, including a new roof constructed from stone quarried from the estate. The mill became operational and first ground flour in October 2009 when it was officially opened by HRH The Prince of Wales.

The mill pond and rear view of the Mill.

Water comes from Lidcombe Wood, is diverted to form the mill race, then directed in to the pond via a sluice and spillway at the entrance. Water then enters the back of the Mill on the second floor level. The Mill can operate for approximately 4 hours before the water in the pond is exhausted.

The entire operation is water-powered. Water from the mill pond flows through a launder, or trough; then a penstock, or sluice, controls the flow over the 24ft diameter wheel to rotate it clockwise. The wheel is the 8th largest in England. A horizontal shaft drives the sack hoist, elevator and drive to the grading machine, or sieve.

A one tonne bag of grain grown on the estate is sucked into the bin.

Grain from the grain bin then goes into the hopper supervised here by volunteer Adrian Sharpe, and then into the shoe.

The shoe, the tapering trough which feeds grain into the eye of the stones, is agitated by the damsel, a contraption which causes the shoe to wobble, shaking and controlling the amount of grain flowing to the mill-stones - too much clags the stones, too little is not good for the stones either.

The 48" diameter stones are French burr-quartz. Flour falls off the edge of the stones and is sent by the sweeper through the shute, which is manually controlled by a shutter, into the wholemeal bag of flour. Wholemeal is the first grading.

 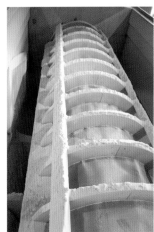  

The ground flour travels by elevator and is then fed by gravity into the grader. There are three grades of mesh: fine, middling and coarse. The miller Mike Lovatt changes full bags of the three different grades of flour which are then hoisted to the middle floor.

Robin Rogers weighs up the flour into 1.5kg bags for domestic use, and 16kg or 25kg bags for caterers.

Fields of buttercups evoke childhood memories of arriving at the village school with pollen like gold-dust on our shoes....

THE MILLINER

Louise Pocock has established her millinery business in Chipping Campden High Street.

The creative process starts with a basic moulded straw or felt bucket shape. This is steamed, blocked over a form, stiffened and trimmed. The edges are hand-wired and the bands and embellishments are entirely hand-stitched.

Louise also works with sinamay and jinsin materials, versatile natural fibres with different weaves and textures which are used to create incredible shapes.

Many of her unique and eye-catching hats have been designed for Cheltenham racegoers, and one of her fedoras features in a famous advertising campaign starring a zebra....

The hallowed ruins of Hailes Abbey, the 13th century Cistercian monastery which was a holy and revered pilgrimage destination until the Reformation and Dissolution of the Monasteries overseen by Henry VIII in the 16th century.

FARMCOTE

Dawn breaks over the old pilgrim track from Hailes Abbey which was laid by the monks of the Abbey themselves, along the Cotswolds escarpment to the chapel of ease at the tiny hamlet of Farmcote.

Dedicated to St. Faith, the chapel occupies an elevated, peaceful spot overlooking the Severn Vale. Medieval pilgrims would rest here on their way to visit the famous phial of holy blood at Hailes Abbey.

The squint in the east wall of the chapel allowed lepers and other 'undesirables' to watch the service from the outside without coming into contact with the rest of the worshippers.

The communion table at the end of the nave is topped with a large 13th century stone mensa, or altar slab, which has five crosses carved into the surface symbolising the five wounds of Christ. Such altars were removed from all churches during the Reformation; however, this one survived and was reset during restoration work in 1891.

FARMCOTE HERBS AND CHILLI PEPPERS

Farmcote Herbs and Chilli Peppers are located in an enviable spot high up in the Cotswold Hills near Winchcombe, with fabulous panoramic views across the vale to the Malvern Hills and the Black Mountains of Wales. Owners Jane and Tim have developed their hobby of growing herbs and chilli peppers and transformed it into a thriving business.

The selection of culinary and medicinal herbs includes basils, corianders, dill, borage, tarragons, oreganos, and many more.

They grow more than 30 different chilli peppers, from mild to medium to very hot, and as well as selling plants they stock chilli chutneys, salsas, dips, oils and chocolate, and chilli sausages and burgers supplied by Sudeley Hill Farm.

Over August Bank Holiday Jane and Tim host a Chilli Festival, when numerous stalls provide a wide range of chilli products and refreshments for the many visitors.

The view from Farmcote, the epitome of an "Area of Outstanding Natural Beauty."

FLOWER CONFETTI

Ribbons of vibrant multi-coloured larkspur drift away into the distance on the Wyke Manor Estate near Pershore. Owner Charles Hudson's family have been farming here for more than 250 years. By way of diversification they grow 15 acres of flowers, all from seed, to produce beautiful natural confetti.

Hundreds of thousands of flowers are hand picked here every Summer; here, cornflowers are being harvested and put into cardboard boxes.

Larkspur, or delphinium, covers a spectrum from white to pink to blue to violet....the white are always the last to bloom. Shakespeare referred to them as "Lark's Heel" in his poem "Bridal Song."

The splendid Wyke Manor was given to Catherine Parr as a present from Henry VIII, whom she married in 1543.

The stems of larkspur are placed in vases and then left for the petals to dry and drop naturally.

The petals are mixed by hand to bespoke requirements. They are sold by the pint loose, or in individual sachets, and sent all over the world.

Because they are biodegradable, and therefore environmentally friendly, the petals are perfect for wedding confetti. The Company has provided petals for thousands of weddings, including those of celebrities and Royalty, and they have also been used in films, TV and for many other occasions.

The beautiful village of Blockley attracts large numbers of ramblers who delight in exploring the winding footpaths and the Blockley Brook as it ripples through the valley.

SHOE MAKING

Bill Bird has been making shoes in his Northwick Business Park workshop since 1988. Using best quality materials, Bill and his small dedicated team of skilled craftsmen produce bespoke and orthopaedic shoes and boots for clients who are unable to wear off-the-shelf footwear.

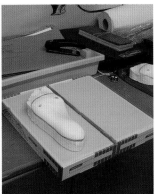

Once the client's requirements and measurements have been discussed, plaster casts of the feet are made.

From these, Bill hand-carves the last on which the shoe will be fashioned - he is one of only four craftsmen in the country skilled in hand-carving lasts.

Kirsty Procter is cutting and making patterns, supervised by Roberta the cat!

Emily Jewett is "clicking out," that is, cutting the leathers for the uppers.

Becky Thorn is finishing the edges and soles; she specialises in designing and making soles and heels.

Russell Marks is responsible for "closing" assembly and fine stitching of the different sections of the uppers. This involves both machine and hand-stitching.

After soaking, the insole is left on the last to dry.

The upper is secured onto the last and left to settle for several weeks, which is how the shoe takes shape.

Kirsty pulls out the rivets ready for the "try on" stage.

Each client needs four visits to the workshop: on the third visit a false heel is fitted to the shoe, which can be adjusted to determine a correct fit.

Over the years many happy clients have left the workshop with a spring in their step – a perfectly fitting shoe can greatly improve mobility and sense of well-being. Bill and his team have also made footwear for clients at Headley Court, the Armed Forces dedicated rehabilitation centre.

The finished shoe: a remarkable piece of teamwork!

The Secret Garden at Campden House is open to the public as part of the National Gardens Scheme, and annually to raise funds for the Red Cross.

This charming cottage garden belongs to an original burgage plot in Chipping Campden. These long narrow plots were introduced in medieval times and can be identified by their dimensions being measured in perches (5.5 yards). This plot runs from the property frontage in the High Street right through to Back Ends at the rear.

THE CART WASH

The Cart Wash before restoration.

With the disappearance of horse drawn carts and wagons from the rural scene, the 19th century Cart Wash in Chipping Campden fell into disrepair. But in 2015, thanks to the generosity of townsfolk and a band of local volunteers, it was cleared of grass and weeds, enabling the original stone walls, floor and drain to be repaired and restored by builder Nick Godson.

In Winter the carters used the Wash to clean mud off the cartwheels, while in the dry Summer months the cart would be left standing in the water - this was important so that the wheels could expand, thus preventing the spokes from working loose which could lead to the iron tyre falling off.

Spring water was pumped to the Wash from the Conduit House on the hill above Westington, which also supplied the Almshouses.

This two wheel tip cart was built in Paxford by Don Keyte Senior for well-known local farmer and benefactor Fred Badger. He would have used it for carting fodder such as mangolds to the livestock on his farm at Lapstone.

STONE CARVER

Ian Ashurst was a BBC drama production designer for 30 years before moving to Chipping Campden to pursue a new career in stone carving.

Starting with detailed drawings he uses his artistic skill and technical know-how to create a whole range of unique pieces in stone - stone sculptures, carvings in relief, and carved lettering for house signs and suchlike.

His craft perfectly complements the Cotswold landscape in which he works and finds his inspiration.

The marker stone for the refurbished Cart Wash is one of Ian's original pieces.

CHAIR MAKING

The medieval-style oak-framed Silkwood Barn at Westonbirt Arboretum.

Here students learn how to select unseasoned timber from the coppiced woodland, cleave it from the log, shape it with side axes and drawknives on a shaving horse, turn legs and spindles on a pole lathe and use various carving tools to make for themselves an elegant Windsor chair, which will last for generations.

LETTERPRESS PRINTING

Letterpress printing is a technique of relief printing using a press; printed copies are produced by repeated direct impression of an inked raised surface against sheets of paper or card.

Despite the now routine use of computerised printing processes, the letterpress is enjoying something of a renaissance: David Lewis at Cherry Press in Chipping Campden's High Street, accredited by the Guild of Master Craftsmen, is reviving this traditional craft.

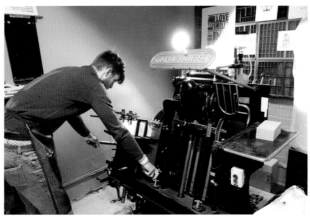 

He uses two vintage presses in his workshop, a Heidelberg Windmill which is fully automatic, and a Crown Folio Arab, which is manually operated (i.e. by applying foot and leg pressure!) - the skill lies in applying just the right amount of force....
In addition he uses a machine for hot-foil printing which operates at 100-150 degrees centigrade.

David and Amie Lewis with their dogs Archie and Merlin in their studio shop where they sell their original stationery, prints and greetings cards.

Originally the process used raised wood or metal type but here David transfers a unique digitally produced design onto a photopolymer plate which creates great detail and effects a deep impression.

The printing ink is mixed by hand using the Pantone colour scale. From the ink duct it passes through five rollers before reaching the main inking cylinder which feeds form rollers.

Burnt Norton in the golden early evening light.

T.S.Eliot, recognised as one of the greatest poets of the 20th century, stumbled across this impressive manor house and gardens while staying with friends at nearby Chipping Campden in the 1930's. The uniqueness and beauty of the gardens in particular inspired him to write the opening poem of his famous work "Four Quartets."

It is on record that T.S.Eliot had a life-long aversion to large animals: one day while walking in the Cotswold countryside he was almost trampled by a lively heifer and only escaped by diving into a bush....... to commemorate the event he wrote an amusing poem for the children of a close friend:

"Of all the beasts that God allows
In England's green and pleasant land,
I most of all dislike the Cows:
Their ways I do not understand.

It puzzles me why they should stare
At me, who am so innocent,
Their stupid gaze is hard to bear -
It's positively truculent."

© The Estate of T.S.Eliot

A muted Autumn sunrise envelops this stubble field near Hidcote in a rosy glow.

This 18th century timber-framed granary at Burmington is supported on limestone staddle stones. These stones lift the building off the ground, thereby protecting the stored grain from vermin or flooding. Hay ricks and game larders were similarly underpinned.

The pitched gables and honey-coloured limestone walls of the classic Cotswold village of Stanton viewed from the famous Mount Inn. The vista rolls out across the Vale of Evesham towards the Malvern Hills and the mountains of Wales.

STANTON

The archetypal Cotswold cottages at Stanton huddle beneath the slopes of Shenberrow Hill. Apart from the occasional coachload of tourists there is little outward sign of commercialisation - even the street lighting is a reminder of an earlier age.

Sir Philip Sydney Stott, a wealthy architect and civil engineer, arrived in the area in the early 20th century, restored Stanton Court and other historic buildings on the estate and is generally credited with revitalising the village. He installed street lamps powered by his own generator at Stanton Court - they are believed to be the first electric street lights in the country and they are still in use today.

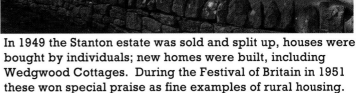

In 1949 the Stanton estate was sold and split up, houses were bought by individuals; new homes were built, including Wedgwood Cottages. During the Festival of Britain in 1951 these won special praise as fine examples of rural housing.

The village cross, built on the wayside to remind travellers of and reinforce their Christian faith as they passed by, dates from medieval times. The sundial at the top is 17th century.

It wasn't until the 13th century that backless stone benches appeared in the nave of churches for general use; prior to that, benches were only placed against the walls and were reserved for the elderly and infirm - hence the expression arose "the weakest go to the wall." This stone bench can be seen in St. Michael's Church.

REMEMBRANCE SUNDAY

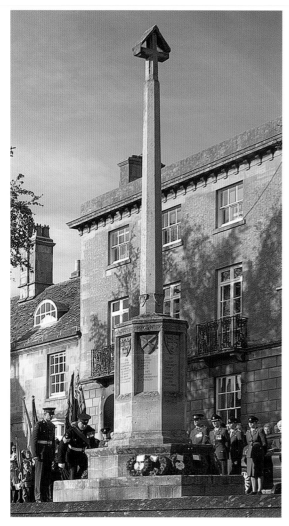

Just a few yards from Broadway Tower is a stone memorial to the crew who perished when their Whitley Bomber, from RAF Honeybourne, crashed while on operational training during World War Two.

An inter-denominational service is held annually at this quiet spot to remember them.

.... lest we forget

"All we have of freedom,
all we use or know -
This our fathers bought for us
long and long ago."

Rudyard Kipling

ARTS AND CRAFTS

The Tower was used as a holiday retreat by the designer and artist William Morris, famous today for his distinctive style of handcrafted products and furnishings. A room in the Tower is dedicated to his designs.

This collection of Arts and Crafts silverware by eminent local silversmiths can be viewed at Court Barn Museum in Chipping Campden.

The magnificent views from Broadway Tower, together with its peaceful yet imposing location, have captivated and inspired many significant artists, writers, craftsmen and film makers over the past two centuries.... on a clear day the views stretch to a 65 mile radius and, remarkably, cover 16 counties.

Several renowned pre-Raphaelite artists spent time at the Tower, among them Holman Hunt, whose allegorical painting "The Light of the World" has influenced the lives of so many people.

Examples of stylish Arts and Crafts era window and door furniture.

YOUNG FARMERS' CLUBS

The National Federation of Young Farmers has a membership of 23,000 young people between the ages of 10 and 26; they are supported and trained in all aspects of farming and the countryside. There are fifteen different clubs in the Gloucestershire Federation.

The North Cotswold contingent of Gloucestershire Young Farmers attends their annual Harvest Thanksgiving at Gloucester Cathedral.

The various clubs in the Gloucestershire Federation meet regularly to take part in inter-club competitions.

Some amusing and imaginative farm machinery created from vegetables....

The photographic competition showcases the artistic talents of the members.

There is fierce competition in the flower-arranging class.

The judges have a tough job deciding on the winners.

Eric Freeman, past County President of the Gloucestershire Federation, admires some of the exhibits. Eric is a well-known and much-loved character in the farming world; he was a founder member of Newent Young Farmers Club back in 1944, and is a lifelong supporter and honorary life governor of the Three Counties Show.

The ability to judge and critically evaluate stock is an important part of the young farmer's development. The guiding principles are to make a judgment by eye and then confirm by careful handling. In competition conditions the young judges have only a few minutes to observe and make their evaluation.

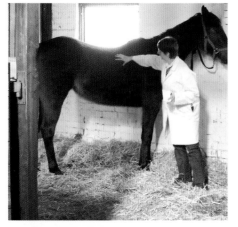

These pigs appear well-balanced and healthy.

The sheep have their teeth, feet and udders checked.

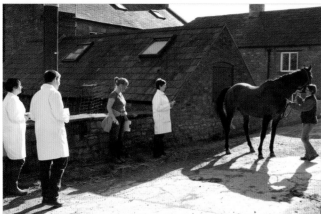

It's important to stand back and have a good look at the horse to observe overall balance and proportion, before getting up close to check feet, teeth, and muscle definition.

The cows must be judged on frame, body condition, mobility, feet and legs, and udder.

The ford and ancient stone clapper bridge cross the gently flowing River Windrush near Kineton, Gloucestershire.

Clapper bridges are the earliest simple stone bridges: they comprise large slabs of stone resting on stone piers to span a stream or small river. This one at Kineton almost certainly dates from medieval times.

WORKING THE LAND

Martin and William Haines are 5th generation farmers, working 2000 acres around Chipping Campden. 800 acres are used for growing vegetables - peas, courgettes, marrows, purple sprouting, fodder beet, potatoes, and Brussels sprouts.

Planting of 10 different varieties of sprouts starts in May - seven rows at a time. Each worker sits with a box of plants in front of him - good teamwork is essential here.

William Haines runs the growing operation of the Farm. Here he checks some of the 200 acres of sprouts for maturity.

The sprouts are supplied exclusively to Marks and Spencer and Aldi supermarkets.

Harvesting starts in early July and continues right through to the second week of April. During the two weeks prior to Christmas the sprouts need to be harvested 24 hours a day to keep up with demand.

Manpower and technology working in harmony: operators feed the entire stem into the machine, where rotating blades strip off the sprouts.

The sprouts are now ready to be moved on to the packing sheds to begin their journey to the supermarket shelves.

Some sprouts are still picked by hand - the leaves remaining on the stems make good fodder for these ewes as they wait the arrival of their lambs. The Farm has some 700 ewes and lambs.

The packing house is run by Martin Haines and his team of around 50 regular staff.

The sprout strippers clean and trim off the outer leaves, and then the sprouts are fed onto a conveyor which moves them on to the machine which puts them into individual bags ready for dispatch to the supermarket.

The packs are labelled.

Quality Control keeps an eye on the team packing purple sprouting.

Asparagus has a relatively short season so occasionally it is necessary for extra supplies to be bought in from other growers - this here was grown in Herefordshire, but packaged by the Haines family.

The distinctive primrose collars on the scarlet jackets of the North Cotswold Huntsmen symbolise the time-honoured traditions which have been passed down to the current generation of devotees.

THE FARMERS' BLOODHOUNDS

The riders enjoy a warming welcome drink in the Courtyard of the Lygon Arms Hotel in Chipping Campden, served by the Potter family: four generations of the family have owned and run the Hotel since 1942.

Bloodhounds hunt "Clean Boot" - that is, they follow the scent of a quarry following a predetermined line. A day's hunting consists of 2 - 3 lines, covering an average of 15 miles.

The Hunt sets off along the Cotswold lanes; the Hunt Masters wear burgundy jackets and etiquette requires the other riders to wear blue, black or tweed.

It is a demanding sport, with a fast pace and many hedges to jump, but there is usually an alternative route for those who feel less brave....

Sunrise over the Stour Valley.

*"And lo! In a flash of crimson splendour,
with blazing scarlet clouds.... heralding his majestic approach
God's sun rises up on the world."*

William Makepeace Thackeray

A gaggle of Canada geese lazes under the dazzling canopy of lakeside copper beeches in the last of the Autumn sunshine.

The gold and crimson colours of Autumn, viewed from Snowshill, across the Broadway valley.

"Go sit upon the lofty hill,
And turn your eyes around,
Where waving woods and waters wild
Do hymn an Autumn sound."

Elizabeth Barrett Browning

RAPESEED OIL PRODUCTION

Harvesting rapeseed at Charlie Beldam's family farm in the Cotswolds.

Once ripe, the rapeseed pods are harvested, the black seed extracted, dried and stored, ready for processing.

THE COLD PRESSING PROCESS

1. Seed is fed from above into the three hoppers of the pressing machine

2. Seed is processed using an Archimedes screw

3. Oil comes out at the base of the screw; the bi-product pellets come out at the front and are sold to local farmers for animal feed

4. Oil passes into a storage container, filtrate powder is added to collect any debris

5. Oil is pumped through filters and collected in the tray below

6. The final filter filters down to 1 micron

Charlie fills the bottles of Cotswold Gold which are then capped and labelled.

Jason Gonifas labels mayonnaise, made in nearby Honeybourne using only natural ingredients and 80% rapeseed oil.

Traditional cold-pressing preserves the natural health benefits of the rapeseed; it extracts 30% of the oil from the seed.

Rapeseed is widely used in all methods of cooking: it is used in mayonnaise, margarine, salad dressings etc. It is low in saturated fat and high in Omega-3, making it an extremely healthy product. Chefs such as Raymond Blanc are supplied by the Company.

Cotswold Gold Extra Virgin Rapeseed Oil has won many prestigious awards. Rapeseed infusions using herbs and spices are also produced.

First light on a frosty November morning, and the sheep are steaming as they near the end of their two mile journey through the town to new pasture.

The lane to Hidcote winds between frothy hoar-frosted hedgerows....

"the brightest hour of unborn Spring...."
Percy Bysshe Shelley

DUMMER BEAGLES

The Dummer Beagles' amazing sense of smell is not diminished by the wintry conditions as they set off enthusiastically on their Boxing Day Meet.

These early lambs and their hungry mothers on the Coneygree waiting patiently for the shepherd's delivery of fresh fodder.

Snowy Broad Campden.

"....the white face of the winter day came sluggishly on, veiled in a frosty mist...."

Charles Dickens